# Little Penny
## Gives, Saves, and Spends

Written by Mark Goldman
Illustrated by Koen Setyawan

Little Penny and her big brother Buck like to visit Nana.

Penny loved helping Nana in her garden.

Nana liked Penny helping her. She gave Penny ten dimes. Penny wondered what she could do with them.

The next day, Penny went shopping with Mom. She saw a toy unicorn and bought it with eight dimes.

Another girl was buying a cowgirl hat but needed more money. Penny helped her by giving her one dime.

At home, Penny remembered the piggy bank that Dad gave her. That was a great place to keep her last dime! Mom and Dad were happy.

Penny kept growing and helping Mom and Dad at home. She was a good helper. They gave her a dollar every week.

Penny got to go to the store sometimes to buy a toy with some of her money.

Sometimes her friend needed money for ice cream. Penny liked helping others.

# Check out Little Penny's brother book!

## Note From the Author

I wrote this book because I was fortunate to have loving parents that taught me the importance of both giving and saving. As far as the spending was concerned, that came naturally.

My hope for the child you are reading this book to is that they will also learn the value of both giving and saving early in life, and that they will develop beneficial habits that stick with them for a lifetime.

May God bless you greatly for reading to this child.

-Mark Goldman

www.give-save-spend.com

published by
**Fox Tales Children's Books**

A division of Our Written Lives, LLC
San Antonio, Texas
www.OurWrittenLives.com

Mark Goldman ©2024
Art by Koen Setyawan

ISBN: 978-1-942923-91-6 (Hardback)

Fonts licensed for commercial use.

www.ingramcontent.com/pod-product-compliance
Lightning Source LLC
Chambersburg PA
CBRC092116280426
43673CB00082B/420